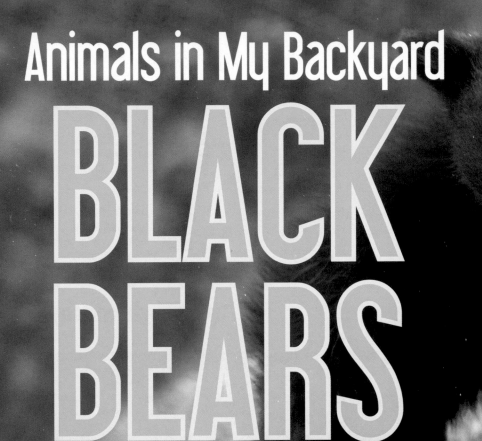

Animals in My Backyard

BLACK BEARS

Pamela McDowell

MEDIA ENHANCED BOOKS
AV2
BY WEIGL
ADDED VALUE · AUDIO VISUAL

www.av2books.com

AV² provides enriched content that supplements and complements this book. Weigl's AV² books strive to create inspired learning and engage young minds in a total learning experience.

Your AV² Media Enhanced books come alive with...

Go to **www.av2books.com**, and enter this book's unique code.

BOOK CODE

U558658

AV² by Weigl brings you media enhanced books that support active learning.

Audio
Listen to sections of the book read aloud.

Video
Watch informative video clips.

Embedded Weblinks
Gain additional information for research.

Try This!
Complete activities and hands-on experiments.

Key Words
Study vocabulary, and complete a matching word activity.

Quizzes
Test your knowledge.

Slide Show
View images and captions, and prepare a presentation.

... and much, much more!

Published by AV² by Weigl.
350 5th Avenue, 59th Floor New York, NY 10118
Website: www.av2books.com www.weigl.com

Library of Congress Cataloging-in-Publication Data

McDowell, Pamela.
 Black bears / Pamela McDowell.
    p. cm. -- (Animals in my backyard)
Includes bibliographical references and index.
ISBN 978-1-61913-267-2 (hard cover : alk. paper) -- ISBN 978-1-61913-271-9 (soft cover : alk. paper)
1. Black bears--Juvenile literature. I. Title.
QL737.C27M358 2013
599.78'5--dc23
                                    2011050247

Printed in the United States of America in North Mankato, Minnesota
1 2 3 4 5 6 7 8 9 0 16 15 14 13 12

022012
WEP020212

Project Coordinator: Aaron Carr   Art Director: Terry Paulhus

Weigl acknowledges Getty Images as the primary image supplier for this title.

BLACK BEARS

CONTENTS

Meet the black bear.

She has thick black fur.
Her thick black fur keeps her warm.

She watches her mother when she is young.

When she is young, she learns how to hunt and fish.

She smells with her large nose.

With her large nose,
she can find food easily.

She digs with her long claws.

With her long claws, she can
dig up plants and turn over logs.

She eats meat with her strong teeth.

With her strong teeth,
she can tear meat and fish.

She uses many different sounds to talk.

To talk, she clacks, grunts, and growls.

The black bear lives
in the forest.

In the forest, there is water
and food close by.

She is safe from snow
and cold in her den.

In her den, she will sleep all winter.

If you meet the black bear, she may be surprised. She might not run away.

If you meet the bear, stay away.

BLACK BEAR FACTS

These pages provide more detail about the interesting facts found in the book. They are intended to be used by adults as a learning support to help young readers round out their knowledge of each animal featured in the Animals in My Backyard series.

Pages 4–5

Black bears are mammals. Mammals are covered with fur or hair. A black bear's fur can be black, brown, or cinnamon-colored to help her blend into her surroundings and hide from danger. Sometimes, black bears can be white. They are often called spirit bears. Black bears are the most common type of bear in North America.

Pages 6–7

Baby black bears learn from their mothers. The mother bear gives birth to two or three cubs during winter. They weigh 7 ounces (200 grams). This is about as much as a juice box. Cubs cannot open their eyes at birth. The mother nurses the cubs until spring. Cubs stay with their mother for two years, learning how to find food, hunt, and fish. When cubs leave their mother, they live alone.

Pages 8–9

The black bear has a large nose. Bears have poor eyesight, but they can smell and hear very well. A black bear will move downwind and stand up on two feet to smell the air. Black bears can smell prey from up to 1 mile (1.6 kilometers) away. Bears use their sense of smell to hunt small animals and find food in the forest.

Pages 10–11

Black bears have long claws. Their claws are also sharp. The bear uses these claws to dig, turn, and lift objects to find food such as ants and other insects. Strong claws also help the bear to climb trees quickly. To escape danger, a cub can easily climb 100 feet (30 m), the height of two telephone poles stacked on top of each other.

Pages 12–13

Black bears have strong teeth. Black bears are omnivores. This means they eat both meat and plants. Strong, sharp teeth help bears chew tough meat and slippery fish. The bear's long tongue helps her eat blueberries, buffalo berries, and ants. To prepare for winter, a black bear may spend up to 20 hours a day eating.

Pages 14–15

Bears talk by making many different sounds. Black bears communicate with sounds and actions. A bear may clack its teeth together, grunt, or growl. If a bear feels threatened, it may shake its head and open its mouth. If it is curious, it might stand up. When in danger, a young cub's cry may sound like a human baby.

Pages 16–17

Black bears live in the forest. Most black bears live in dense forests away from humans. In the forest, there is often water close by. Black bears are good swimmers and will fish in rivers and lakes. Bears may be attracted to campgrounds if food is not put away in a safe place. A bear can easily bite through a cooler to find food.

Pages 18–19

Black bears sleep in a den to stay warm. Black bears live in dens inside caves or under tree stumps. The den protects the bear from bad weather and gives her a place to hibernate during winter. She will stay warm and sleep when food is hard to find. Some bears may spend almost half of their lives in their dens.

Pages 20–21

Black bears are often found in parks and natural areas. Hikers should make loud noises to warn bears that people are near. If people surprise a bear or get between a mother bear and her cubs, the bear may charge. A black bear can run 35 miles (56 km) per hour.

WORD LIST

Research has shown that as much as 65 percent of all written material published in English is made up of 300 words. These 300 words cannot be taught using pictures or learned by sounding them out. They must be recognized by sight. This book contains 47 common sight words to help young readers improve their reading fluency and comprehension. This book also teaches young readers several important content words. These words are paired with pictures to aid in learning and improve understanding.

Page	Sight Words First Appearance
4	the
5	has, her, keeps, she
6	and, how, is, learns, mother, to, watches, when, young
8	large, with
9	can, find, food
10	long
11	over, plants, turn, up
12	eats
14	different, many, sounds, talk, uses
17	by, close, in, lives, there, water
18	from
19	all, will
20	away, be, if, may, might, not, run, you

Page	Content Words First Appearance
4	black bear
5	fur
8	nose
10	claws
11	logs
12	meat, teeth
13	fish
17	forest
18	cold, den, snow
19	winter